TECHNORAGE

TechnoRage

Poems

WILLIAM OLSEN

TRIQUARTERLY BOOKS/NORTHWESTERN UNIVERSITY PRESS

EVANSTON, ILLINOIS

TriQuarterly Books
Northwestern University Press
www.nupress.northwestern.edu

Printed in the United States of America

10 9 8 7 6 5 4 3 2

Library of Congress Cataloging-in-Publication Data
Names: Olsen, William, 1954– author.
Title: Technorage : poems / William Olsen.
Description: Evanston, Illinois : TriQuarterly Books/Northwestern University Press, 2017. |
    Includes bibliographical references.
Identifiers: LCCN 2016049162 | ISBN 9780810135123 (pbk. : alk. paper) |
    ISBN 9780810135130 (e-book)
Classification: LCC PS3565.L822 T43 2017 | DDC 811.54—dc23
LC record available at https://lccn.loc.gov/2016049162

Contents

Acknowledgments

Gratitude to the editors of the following publications, where some of these poems, sometimes in different versions, appeared:

American Literary Review: "The Afterlife of Deer," "Green Flash"

Barrow Street: "Ceasing Never"

Cave Wall: "Desk," "One Question for Ed"

Cerise Press: "Unto," "Watching Glaciers Melt"

Cimarron Review: "Early Murder," "Leafdom" ("Yellow across rat-gray asphalt . . .")

Columbia Poetry Review: "Saint Lucy's Night"

Court Green: "Foreclosure of the Moon"

Dunes Review: "And the Creatures Lay Down," "Up There"

Hunger Mountain: "Damnation," "Our Heron," "Out of the Vortex"

Numéro Cinq: "Frost at Dawn"

The Ocean State Review: "Customer Service," "Under a Rainbow"

Parthenon West Review: "TechnoRage"

Plume: "Posthumous Cabin," "To Anything at All"

Plume Anthology 3: "Seasons of the Day"

Plume Anthology 4: "Coyote after Field Fire"

Poetry in Michigan / Michigan in Poetry: "Leafdom" ("These leaves are neither poems . . .")

Saint Elizabeth Street: "A Natural History of Silence"

Third Coast: "My Middle Name"

Thanks to Beckian Fritz Goldberg, Brandon Krieg, and David Wojahn for their help and support. Thanks to Parneshia Jones for her editorial guidance and steadying grace. Thanks always and especially to Nancy Eimers.

TECHNORAGE

Posthumous Cabin

And got away to it, and left the work to others
maybe twice a year for a couple-few weeks,
and sat inside, and drove from, and took walks
and sat on boulders like life was all easy chairs.

And in comfort wrote some things down as from deep inside
that we might describe how obvious beauty is
and the reader fall away from his confusing surroundings,
and join us in the cabin, yet keep a distance.

And for most of the year that cabin was quiet
whereas the lake had everything and more to say.
Its breakers unscrolled day after day
whether anyone was there to read such scrolls.

And mostly there was reading inside a cabin:
an ideal, a fixed notion of such shelter as
admitted the elemental just enough, and no more.
Mostly we didn't think about the cabin.

And shouldn't we have put our memories to better use
in seeing them forward in the medium of poetry
waiting to see where we were going with it,
holding its breath on our account, or the shore's?

And if the lake was going to die, at least the shore
grew over with bristling cottonwood saplings
rooted to sludge—acrid sun-bleached algae.
The dock was a gangplank to water too shallow to drown in.

And the canoe remained upside down all year round,
and the whole enterprise of saying something with decency
never seemed quite heartwarming enough once
the climate of our opinion also started warming.

And the ironies that rendered our voices naive—
soft flames, our lightsome voices, pilot lights—
did we think we owned the world we (selflessly?) feared for,
each alone, yet more and more mutually frightened?

And if I was running from myself and you from yourself,
the clouds were blowing away too quickly for either of us
to fasten them on paper or on a screen
that ended atop the heap of a toxic waste site.

And even when it was not too late, we both foundered,
obsessed with everything that was least about life,
the chasms and the Armageddons owing to untold grief,
what God shat: the stupefying self-and-earth extinctions.

And for all and anything about life there was plenty of,
the simplicity, the obvious extraordinariness,
these the machines consigned to oblivion.
Yet we could still get truly and even wholly lost.

I

Desk

Every thing
I say of the world
is less true of
the world

than of myself.
The desk
is a timetable,
a cliff to lean

my elbows on,
a boat to rock
asleep in, a night
in the open.

I'm having
to show up
and sit down
to hear out

whether to sleep
or reach down into
the wake of
these others.

Customer Service

This guy at the counter today, tousled hair, eyes darting then holding
like epitaphs do to their gravestones, face like a cracked baseball glove
after so many catches and flubs and so many despondent benched innings,
he's saying to me, sensing my impatience that if it could
would annihilate anything in its way, "Go ahead of me,
I'm just getting my things together," and there I am at the head of the line
pulling out of my pocket some small change to make things
easier for a smiling clerk—the name on her tag says SHARON,
Sharon who restores instant hope of us who stand in line waiting,
Sharon who will never hear her name spoken by me even once.
And now I am stuffing into my pocket—where else?—
some receipt that for all I know has for its final journey
hand to hand, to wallet or pocket, finally to a wastepaper bin
or to a couple of free laundry cycles or to just plain being lost.
The guy at the beginning of a growing line is saying,
"No one else is gonna do it for me," and I'm saying,
"That's for sure, you gotta do everything yourself," he's saying, "That's for sure,"
and then finally saying, "My mama isn't gonna do it for me,"
with some tacit rage of having said that hovering in his face.
Hell yeah, I back off from inside my body to even further inside my body
just so self can be involved, feeling implicated as always
for existing in the first place, navigating its own churning motives.
But what is this self? Do we have to get into that again?
Here is what the self is. It is a grand perhaps, knowing
involuntarily that the words, his, mine, just came out that way,
I could be him absently staring at a retro bubble gum machine,
he could be you, he could be right here reading your querulous story,
someone looking down at you from up here, don't look to me,
don't even look to yourself, the answers are more obvious than we are,
me, him, her, we, them, and, I'm afraid to say to you, I'm relieved
to say to you, what you already know. You. You are anyone else.

The Afterlife of Deer

Anything but unsurprising is
a habit deer have
What they are to me until they happen

in snow/leaf/wind
sun/rain/moon
is nothing if not always serendipitous

In my globe of space and time
they change place with one another That
is what memory is

That is why we die
interchangeable
shadows of scud-clouds scudded across winter's

blade-scraped ice
Heaven is the same
for them

frozen pond
empty swing sets
heaven

*

unfortunate birth
uncontrollable circumstance
heaven

they dream of corn
our underworld
this ice pond

Heaven's roof we walk gingerly upon
or its ceiling cracks
Death is beneath us

Heaven is beneath us
Earth is beneath us
Joy is beneath us Contempt

always looks downward

*

We are told not to feed
Whatever record left behind
only yesterday

the nuanced tilt of the two halves
of the hoof prints
whatever thought them up

not all that mindful
The oaks start bearing
Pea-sized acorns

cut down on predators
there is no other choice but life and more life
or less

and let the animals starve
and not to feed
just watch That was what our life was

*

Their tracks get all mixed up for us
for us their silence is
unheard of

a time before paradise or loss
that calm of theirs good sense
Best to go unseen

How have their carcasses been disposed
You can't see hear
you can't even smell

                          *

Did I tell you about three of them
the family I talked to
as to pets or children

baby talk what I said depending
so little on them
surprise didn't speak a word it washed its hands

Their very appearance is a cliff
I walk off
and fall to earth and live to tell their story

My memory
is a thief and my imagination
an undertaker

some family
surprised
unmoving

One Question for Ed

Are words all there are for crying out loud, all the great and
good and lesser books, ballads, screeds, prayers, deeds,
constitutions, obits, wedding notices, birth notices,
evictions, letters, e-mails, bills, phone calls, last cries, first
babbles, chants, recipes, warrants, epitaphs, eulogies,
revelations, no matter how complex, how lyrical, how
moving, how true, the brightest sentences, the most pellucid
paragraphs, the most effulgent chapters, all of Proust a
winsome chandelier, Hemingway a hotel sconce or two,
Bashō one lit match the wind cannot blow out and then it
does, a mockingbird's manic samplings mostly erasure while
I read some Whitman and then the pastor reads from
scripture the part about the garden at the end of Revelations,
in the middle of the City of God, Who said, let there be
light, who was God talking to, Himself, Nancy crying in
near silence, her whole family quieted for once, Nancy, her
mother and her sister and her brother heads bowed down
like daffodils through all the words?

Out of the Vortex

Gust smattered gobs of snow glommed to spruce
limbs
    shingled white, then, through snow fume, a hint
of living green,
        the ecstatic without the static, without confines.
    Outline is idea, any process is arriving at a humble
clump of words,
        so if I say I'm down on my knees what ceiling,
        what hands take mine and pull me to my feet?

                    *

What fashioned the soft blue tree shadows—no,
not shadows,
        wisps of night across day heedlessly laid down,
        whatever these are, a gladness I am otherwise.
    Humankind hidden, hypothetical as slurred trees
down street,
        no shape is but that necessity strictly conforms,
no one
        walks into the eyes, nothing out there to kneel.

                    *

Cut and dried aesthetics, art at its most frugal
        the universalizing principality of smother-love—
some universalizing thief
        has taken all the fine detail away, as proof
        that we've always been losing our memories,
        white drop cloth over sidewalks, driveways,
        abstract forms—balustrades on fence posts.

*

Thrown pots on lampposts, pedimented flat roofs,
eaves
    beveled to bedding for the wind's insomnia,
    bushes—overstuffed sofas—plush cushions
on car tops,
    the un-dug-out cars awaiting derelict orders,
    marmoreal empire—what absentee would want
to rule
    this inhospitably over the upholstery of the air—

*

Hedges are blizzard-coral, a great reef crystallizes,
cold sunlight
    screened is arctic-aquatic now, under an ice cap
we live,
    even breath asphyxiates, even its own passing, nether
shadows.
    Silted earth's ghost—a heavily, indrawn vagary—
    drew frost-graffiti'd windows, specifics randomly
stippled—
    that there is subject to this the human wish.

*

What of those leery leather oak leaf gloves no one
wears,
    who would go out in this would become statue,
    sculptured marble, I can't make out the sign or name
of my own street,
    who would pull me over them like a sweater,
    who would like to be undergone gone under.

*

Footprints shallow, a pathetic picket deer fence
snow picketed with less precision than the fence,
similitude, what a sham, it sculpts no clear edge,
rounded is edge, what a beautiful sham is this,
do you see,
    the blind eyes of the neighborly windows,
    it must be dark inside the average houses,
    indefinite all day rends and shrills this squall,
you want that?
    Do you really think you know who we are?

*

    What of the fictive emptiness, what is purpose
down here,
    snow, that which surrounds me, you You,
    you are not a curtain I or we need to open.
    The neighbors occupy the world they seem,
    Eyesight falls so far in me, my happiness
no need to touch my flesh or hers, that, her shining face,
    not today, this another sort of surrender,
    midafternoon I lie down in my warmth.

*

    Bushes tabletopped and then tented over,
    three juncos dart in and out of one of the gaps,
    two come back out, but I have seen more go in
than go out,
    go into a permeable enclosure there.
    It must be better altogether like that.

*

These branches more than half draped white
and shouldering more snow than branch,
the snowfall so hoisted above more-of-the-same
is lifted up,
    held up into you and from these eyes.
    Whatever you see, I would like to say
    whatever you make of this I would make yours,
    whatever we look out on and we abide
    be lifted up, for the beautiful is ours.

Our Heron

Observation isn't serious play. It is living serious. Same heron. It's used to us, we are as twilight. When we walk down shore. Hand me the binoculars. I'll hand them back. No I can see it with my naked eye. Cup your ear. Drink what I say. Because what was that last squabble about? If we draw too near the heron it will go, meaning that for it we will have gone.

I can't see it every day all day. Sunlight has nothing to do with our sharing the sight of it. I want twilight. A heron is a "how to" book on twilight. Open anywhere. "How to" is a lonely phrase. Lonely is a start. Try saying so. Try making up and try inconclusion. Try twilight.

Then try reading a book so good that every page is dog-eared and you know how safe the heron out there in the reeds feels just about now. Each twilight try the same heron the shade of twilight. Twilight hushes to such tones you have to look so carefully at what you see you become hushed yourself. Then a heron. Pulled forward by fish, the baiting saint of the shallows. Its elongated neck tapers to the beak that always precedes head and eye and ears, the beak being both an emissary for and a tender of the senses.

Sometimes behind slender reed it would vanish to sight, we couldn't make it out, and trying to was like trying to interpret a flyleaf.

For twenty-odd minutes we'd watch for the heron while we brushed mosquitoes from one another's faces. The mosquitoes would have drowned in our hearts if they could have.

Damnation

I kinda like this one, Bob. Leave it.
—The Joker, Gotham City Flugelheim Museum,
Batman (1989)

Francis Bacon's *Figure with Meat*. On both sides of a man seated in a chair as black as can be is a side of meat, hanging wondrously, without hooks. They could be the plucked, flensed wings of an angel. Angels, those birds without trees, nests, or eggs. That man is stationed inside what through the stilled, troubled medium of precise obscurity appears to be an ever receding hallway. Perhaps the ever receding hallway is the negative space behind all canvases. Perhaps this man is fasting. If this man were in the light, what would he do? He ate what is dead and he is alive. He's seated on the throne to interiority. What an atrocious kingdom. It is as postmodern as Abu Ghraib. His head should be a skull. Three holes: two eyes and the lurid gray slur of a mouth. If he is screaming, his scream is a gagged quiet. Get your eyes down on their hands and knees. Pray, weep. Be skinned alive.

The Afterlife of Deer

Harvest midnight
Carcass strung up on a basketball hoop
is still twirling

Harvest bleeds
gyres
on driveway

the sun shining down Where you are
they are
never to be lost or found

no ghost with pen can put to speech or song
one who looked up at me
from the golf course

through the windshield of my moving car
made eye contact and held it
and looked and looked

Memory drove away

*

sight of tongue
sleight of eyes
To disappear only to reappear

Key deer all trust and littleness
shying almost
right up to us

in a dream they showed up dark green
bleeding sap
from the teeth of a backhoe

And did I tell you about the
one just
outside

I was the guy
whose office window that one walked by
like I wasn't there

indifferent if from many singled out
one of those heavenly days
glorious enough to die

*

Deer grazing up in the clouds
able to bear
them

Look up there
Up there
are spring flowers and overgrazing and harvest

Not so near nor so far
No ghost pen can put to tune or speech
wind both fierce and light

Grazing on snow falling upwards
for all I know
All I know

hurts and the afterlife
of a world of hurt
lets me near them

*

Above that you are able
to escape That You Are
or may be able to bear

the one that walked out of the scrub
across beach front right
up to lake was no longer a cherub with antlers

and bent down as if
it were itself an if
and lowered a head as an if

and drank from the if-ebb
It might have been a ghost
Alive still or probably not

death doesn't have a prayer

TechnoRage

If I could walk there or note it on a laptop
it wasn't me—
that false loosestrife was many fruited, and jewelweed was the same
as fireweed.

My wife reads books on clouds
that wander lonely or out loud.
What forms inhabit the sky rain a little heaven across
gnarled vineyards—

it is the spell of sensations
that keep our observations
going, enough that whole days we walk out of each other's
minds.

Dead mole on the state park road, plump little comma
without a sentence.
Overhead the same five herons
day after day surprise me anew.

I've seen this family flap out from the cattails and rushes.
They disregard my regard.
Saying so is a way to remain.

Waxwing, pass me a berry.
I'm hungry and the bladder campions are too many invasive footnotes
to look up.
The definition of realism—

which is all in the margins
when night settles herons
and moonlight takes the thrilled lake for a last little ride—
is glossophilia.

Seaside goldenrod, golden Alexanders.
Best yet, oyster plants gone to zany seed—
terrestrial starbursts, these goatbearded clusterfucks somehow radiate:
"human happiness

will destroy the earth," Albert Schweitzer said of amateur naturalists.
As for silence,
it doesn't exist, concluded John Cage, in his own nearly endless
book—

whatever silence isn't
I want a little bit of.
And as for darkness,

"We're lost if the lights go out,"
Tanizaki Jun'ichirō, once electric light abolished darkness
in Japanese interiors,
In Praise of Shadows.

The heron cast no shadows that far up; down here
I am afraid to be afraid.
I might miss something, something that misses
me.

In the flicker of gaslight
families were destroyed.
Soon, out of the board feet that was Nottingham Forest, in that barrens,
replaced by their children,

factory workers plotted before they were hunted down.
Luddites. First to be called "frame breakers."
Soon it was a capital offense to break a loom.

Man created the machine in his own image.
As for the soul,
"I think that this is something we know exactly
nothing about"—

John Muir—whom Emerson, after a transcontinental ride
a private coach, met and praised,
"a thinking man."

"Thought without reverence
is barren," abstruse Carlyle.
Come any thought but silent spring, please, I'll get down
on my knees

in the lake shallows.
It's *all* deep ecology.
The lake at its lowest level in decades is beaching
the pleasure boats.

Machinery spewing out machinery, the *Transformers* movies,
digitalized visuals
sensational on polyethylene screen
in a climate-controlled environment.

The term "environment" is used here sentimentally.
What the audience sees is irrelevant; what is relevant is that human
forms
sit in a darkness made comfortable by Freon

in chairs designed to maximize comfort
at minimal cost, pleasure goers in rows—
escaping work, or home, unwittingly supporting an industrialized
aesthetics—

"the human frame / A mechanized automaton," Shelley wrote,
"Scarce living pulleys of a dead machine . . ."
"Men are more easily made than machinery," Lord Byron, for a brief
period outraged.

Say yes to cyberutopia
and instant democracy.
Idolized Keats was actually not wealthy enough to vote.

"Poor lonely worshipper"—Muir said of his self.
Bishop pitied the obsessed, her own unlikely nature,
"poor bird," lonely, worshipful—herself—her sandpiper, her fish,
her moose.

"Computer banks have become our nature," Lyotard wrote
of the postmodern condition.
Server farms take up four percent of this nation's unlimited
power.

It's night in the restaurant dumpsters.
It's worse tonight than night somewhere because the War
is right here on our screens.
The bombs are bombing the bombs.

So we can despise all of creation.

Foreclosure of the Moon

Shit slams into it
all the time I
know what that looks like
I have a window

to a white washed
blue jean
day moon what a
gyp of a vision

no one needs
except to
open our minds
to poverty

perfected even the
poor are out of
the picture not
a houseplant

or a spider's
good sense
to hang to What's
to be done

with the human the
mechanical
reproduction of anything
that is human

war on leaves
get the leaves
out of here
houses just keep

pushing the sea
into itself it is
only human to watch
sea push back

same breaking
old sea wind
hard over street same
old cold

up there
ours to say why we fear
distance
ours to say why

when we fear the cold
we fear ourselves
where are the controls
to turn that off

Last of May

White throats
   the last of you
      gone

Wasp on the door screen
   taking the day
      off

your compound eyes
   compound squares
      wings enfolded

like hands in prayer
   or hands in love
      or hands of a corpse

your six legs straddling wire
   no
      just their tips

your hold
   holds
      You scare me

then you are gone too soon
   wasp—
      bless you

waves I love
   to hear
      return night whole

semis
   all-nighters
      driving the distances sane

Under a Rainbow

—Don't be afraid to be naive.

I was driving down a ribbon of road
black as a rifle barrel,
what sunlight showed
light rain put in peril.

This life was a long time
to have to live anything.
Every breath had become a crime
against everything.

A watercolor draft, a faint wonder
arced over a county road.
I could have driven under
not over it—it kneeled

or seemed to in a baize field
same as the field before
then in a brand-new same old field
startled me even more,

instantaneous and always
just around the bend
about to rematerialize
as if I had to pretend

to be something other than sad
on some obscure county road—
there were potholes to relive,
then the beautiful to forgive

as if beauty would never learn
and truth would never lapse—
now arcing over a swaybacked barn
a straw would collapse.

A little rainbow—hardly real
nothing—yet—here—and I—
I made myself up—whereas it was real
in the shallows of the sky.

Again, again, here, then not much—
nothing at all . . . power lines
strung from crutch to crutch.
Earth appeared to be broken.

It blew my sanity away.
It blew utterance away.
It blew my friend Saint Francis away.
One crow flew away,

a scrap of life for eyes to clutch
frozen in the head,
like a spark from the blackest match
that flickers dead.

Which is finally how it goes
for everything in this place
whenever a hard wind blows
as if through human space

where there's always tomorrow,
always a crow for a brother,
always more debt to borrow,
another foreclosure, another.

That every frost had turned to loss,
orchard trees, crowns rusted red,
grazing fields once emerald as moss,
rust on the springs of a bed

thrown outdoors for homeless ghosts.
Worse off lost than dead,
rusted fence wires, rusted posts,
sunflowers with rusted heads,

rust itself rusting, corrosive loss—
splendid, real, miserable—
its own prodigal witness,
miraculous, banal, cruel.

Sun dropped through a slit in the clouds
like a coin into a slot
and the fields shone green,
more lovable than not,

some shocks standing tall,
others broken at the knees,
too busted, almost, to fall,
stunned, numbered clarities.

Some shining, some answering,
over the hills and road,
corn shocks sunning,
almost looking proud—.

Out of the car, along a dune,
after a mile or two
wind through grass whistled
sharper than keening or rue.

Waves breaking—marmorial—
over far out from shore,
waves breaking—funereal—
never reach the shore.

Waves breaking, they're over my head,
my comprehension—poor
waves breaking inside my head
can't hurt me anymore.

Over and over, the same old way
repaving mile by mile,
blue as the sky on the brightest day
memory thinks awhile.

Field by field it reappeared,
field by field as if retold,
then vanished as the road neared
a stand of ashes last year's winds had felled.

Stunted, bent over—
there it was again,
earthly, heavenly, rich, poor,
here, there, and then

some memory you can't get right
so it visits you again
and it just keeps repeating itself,
like it wanted to have a friend.

If the leaves happen to be thronging
down we try to say why
the past should feel like belonging
when it keeps throwing itself away,

and if the same old longing
we have to let die
lapses to a sense of belonging,
just try to say why.

Go figure. This song, it's done.
The clouds know how to hang and move on.
A rainbow and me on the run—
another bright day was gone.

My Middle Name

The Midwest is part of the ether of childhood for me. That is, its insubstantiality still has the power to knock me off my feet.

I was born in Omaha, Nebraska, birthplace of Weldon Kees and death place of Red Cloud. Home, at the beginning of his performing career, to Johnny Carson, whom my father as a young member of a business group watched doing magic tricks. And, at the beginning of his acting career, to Henry Fonda, who my mother remembers lived in a little studio apartment near her parents' home: in her memory he was an artist type, rumored by the local girls to have sketched nudes of models in that studio. Birth, death, sons of immigrants, entertainment for the masses, art for the sake of Eros: the heart of the heart of the heartland. And, at the very center of my imagination then and now, the stockyards where my father worked, smelling to the high heavens of future good red beef for America. And impossibly and logically in the center of these stockyards, Johnny's Café, that haven of cleanliness and homeyness and culinary virtue as my family knew it: you see it in the very opening of the movie *About Schmidt*: it's the venue for the glum retirement party of Warren Schmidt as played by Jack Nicholson. For my family, the Midwest ended where the Great Plains began, in North Platte, just north of which, in the sixties, you could still view wagon-wheel ruts from the Oregon Trail.

I do not wish to break the spell nostalgia has over me: it's too easy to let go of the past as it is.

During a recent phone call my father revealed to me that the source of my middle name, Curtis, was another famous onetime resident of Omaha: the genius behind the air force as we now know it and its first admiral, the first commander of Strategic Air Command (SAC), the hero of the World War II air campaign in Japan who won the loyalty of his men by always flying first in bomber formations, the probable source for both General Jack Ripper as played by Sterling Hayden and the eponymous paraplegic played by Peter Sellers in Stanley Kubrick's *Dr. Strangelove*, and an unsuccessful vice presidential candidate (alongside George Wallace) in 1968: the great American and proud Ohioan Curtis LeMay.

Curtis LeMay's contribution to that campaign, a bid for American voters too conservative for Richard Nixon's placating campaign promise to end the Vietnam War, was the famous line "We'll bomb 'em back to the Stone Age!" His signal contribution to world peace was the military philosophy of MAD, or Mutual Assured Destruction. His strategic achievements included the fire-bombing of Tokyo. He was a primary advocate for the dropping of Fat Man on Nagasaki. He didn't like chaplains waiting on the air fields in England offering final prayers or last rites: he said it set the wrong tone for the day, he'd send the clergymen back to the barracks. He was in agreement with Ralph Nutter, a lead navigator and close friend, who once was overheard saying, "I'm going to grease my guns . . . that's the only religion these goddamn Nazis know!"

One's heritage, when it is not downright absurd, is confounding. But I feel no anguish over my middle name. The past disowns us soon enough. It was only a chance memory in a chance phone call that presented me the source of my middle name. My father can be tough, but he is also a good man and a gentle soul. During that phone call he explained to me that I received my middle name because he and my mother would often see Curtis LeMay at professional softball games in Omaha and because this was the man who made peace, and a free world in the 1950s, and the birth of my older brother and me, possible.

And what can my heritage say to absolve my nominal complicity in our country's first taste of a realizable apocalypse? When I get too pious for my paci-fist britches, I can now summon the radioactive facts and with the full force of my middle name—with me standing in for Slim Pickens and riding a hydrogen bomb while waving a cowboy hat—come plunging down on Premier Kissoff's Doomsday Machine and on all I love and know the best.

On the pig farms of Iowa that fascinated me in childhood vacations from Park Forest—where I grew up—to Omaha. On the shocks of corn of Illinois field that rattled like skeletons. On the fireflies we prized and caught in mason jars for that suffocating light. On Route 30, the first highway to span the coun-try, and on Western Avenue, the longest avenue in the world my father liked to tell the family, and on our family's prefab house maybe a quarter mile from the junction of the two. On memories themselves. On the plot of dirt-clod ground that was our property and that I remember our family visiting on our first visit from Omaha to the prototypical suburb where we would live: our future, a vacant space where our house did not yet stand, so many hundred square feet stringed off by kite string, me holding, I kid you not, a toy model of a B-17, the famed Flying Fortress that probably defeated the Germans in World War II and that Curtis LeMay himself pioneered.

On the four of us, my mother and my father and my brother and me, gazing through nonexistent windows out upon a green fringe, cattails and sumac and milkweed and prairie grass and the few stately oak trees that preceded Park Forest and were absorbed—or obliterated—into its name.

On our nation's crown jewel of defense, Omaha's SAC, fact and fiction: on the buildings and outbuildings that kept my uncle Jack, an electrician, employed after World War II; and on Kubrick's set of the SAC War Room, with its slogan signs PEACE IS OUR PROFESSION, EXTREME WATCHFULNESS, TOTAL COMMITMENT and with its "human reliability tests" that failed to keep the world from ending on the big screen and only hastened the faceless voiceless credits and that unforgettably insipid British version of the love song "We'll Meet Again."

There are so many endgame scenarios—hard to choose one!—now that could come out of the future we don't know we have in us. But first it is time for a digression.

Recently I came across hundreds of letters, stored in a moving box, I wrote to my wife, my then girlfriend, during our college years. One of these letters contains my earliest extant poem, a mutter of prose. It's untitled (I reproduce a cut I apparently made):

> I experienced the marriage of heaven and hell today when
> the xxxxxxxxxxxxxxxxxx radio tuning got stuck between
> a rock station and a religious station. It was a screeching
> sound.

What can I say? Is this premiere poem thoroughly (yes) banal? It is surely succinct and just as surely contemptuous. I remember the drive that occasioned this verbal outing. The song on the pop station was '70s sludge, "Dream Weaver," by Gary Wright: "Driver take away my worries of today/and leave tomorrow behind." Of the sermon that was on the radio station I do not remember a word. The static between the two stations was the takeaway. It was more of a cackle, like a stack of Bibles on fire, like a cathedral on fire, like libraries on fire—something like that.

I was on the freeway late at night, driving through Kansas to see my parents in Oklahoma City and to work there at the Wilson and Company's meat-packing plant, the nation's then second largest, my father then oversaw. I was in a church-white Ford Galaxie 500, an old '60s model. Even then, though, its dashboard seemed intergalactic. The radio got stuck between two stations, and the airwaves went static. I must have wanted to tell of this instant in the middle of nowhere on an interminable night when I couldn't even think to talk or hear an actual human voice for miles upon hundreds of miles. Between stations was a grating pandemonium. Driving across east Kansas at night felt like being on another planet. I had been vacantly watching industrial cornfields lit on and off by headlights. I recall the little clearing the headlights made on the asphalt, a moving pool of light.

I could see the road immediately before me and at any given moment where the highway bent and the headlights swerved off their paths, the top of stalks and ghostly tassels of corn. As far as the headlights shone into was a husbanded creation. All the way up to the sky sloped vast regimental lines of feed corn that would be cows that would be mass-produced teachers and students and magicians and actors and movie makers and electricians and fathers and mothers and brothers, hundreds of millions of us. I was driving under the heavens my namesake had tamed.

Watching Glaciers Melt

My father bought us this trip, he'd taken it, he wanted to give us an experience,
our eyes to see for ourselves a grandeur he felt for a first and last time.

But no one would wish to spend all that long here stranded in the sublime.
Finally, wholly, indiscriminately, it isn't perception that annihilates nature

but species-feverish motion. I could get to love plodding observations.
Gulls ride ice floes for as long as they have till the shadows eagles make

must signal them away so they don't need to turn around to the eagle,
just lumber off, glide idly back, just as, with less frequency, the same eagle does.

I'm brought around to the fears I have created, hoards of my own problems
if only to have reasons to return to with renewed belief in recurrence,

which depends on inexorable inconclusion, sheer, thunderous disruption.
Liner lumbering clockwise, just the right angle, the here in which we stall—

the walls keep coming down. Lip service to the natural world and the body.
How else do we experience for ourselves some perspective of a "world"

that as opposed to the "earth" is so stupidly, blindly, aggressively humane?
Are clouds the most yielding and therefore lasting forms to possibly be?

While these clouds appear to aspire patiently to see themselves across the sky
we marvel at the light so far north into the night, too unmitigated a joy

to write off too quickly as something banal or not grown-up, unmooring
from a world of deadened responsibilities just waiting behind every door,

the long days widening until the quieting of conscience feels oppressive.
Experienced from inside some absolute motion must be what forever is,

some desire at the center of wonder, some absence at the heart of desire.
Nausea in the Erasmus Room, simulated library, fake books and a trophy globe

that perhaps no one has ever thought to spin as the real globe barrels on
forever in the midst of absences. Not one snowflake knows the absences.

To Anything at All

Our father who is neither ours nor a father but farther and nearer,
another night is here.

But the trees out there didn't make up their lives

any more than I do, and they don't have a prayer
and if they do

I have no ears.

Something, anything, the woebegone inside, says
I must go.

No, stay—where did I think I was anyway?
Age.

I haven't finished untying the knotty lies.

And the sky today is wider than the brain,
as time never was.

Anything at all, you can say anything at all.

You can have me. You can have me. Have me

file the shiv to a key
and from their life sentences in my childhood house
free the good drunk,

my mother, then the good butcher,
my father.

Trees.
Cars crouched like alibis—

nothing appears designed to move

or even shiver.
It is always the instant before I give myself away.

That comes later, when the time has always been.

Before I surrender,
I take everything back.

I even pull my fist
out from the heirloom mirror

that was nailed to the wall.

I vanished only when I walked away from it.

Bright Day of the Body

Perhaps pain is most like love in that it comes and goes of its own accord, as if obeying laws from whose knowledge we remain almost totally shut out.
— DAVID B. MORRIS, *The Culture of Pain*

Pain is a system of warning, a friendly warning. Chronic pain is too friendly. Warning all about itself. In it I understand every outcome in my life and language permits me to compare outcomes in the abstract to the shadows tree limbs cast on my shoulders by the window, the limbs themselves shouldering sunlight. Clearly these particulars do all the important shouldering for me. I feel, even from my loneliness, a distance. Understanding becomes all warning. Some specifics still sound the same as always, like cardinals and their hot-iron scribble. But primarily everything says more is coming. It may wish itself to be otherwise, but chronic pain, like love, gives me more everything it's already given. I begin to reside in a fear I can't frighten myself out of.

———————

So many days fail for being preconception. Intention can only birth intention. To give a full account of even a single particular, one need only exhaustively describe its absence. So I cannot give a full account of chronic pain because I cannot describe its absence. Pain is a form of stubbornness, and love is a form of stubbornness. Who wants both? Who?

Early Murder

You crows in your hullabaloo understand the dead of winter
trees you adorn like Christmas ornaments from Satan's mouth.
It's out of the dark, the way you self-portraits look at me
and fly away like dictionaries in the same language.
But for one another you each have a distinct shiny face of the special
leaf of the little sugar maple, my favorite victim,
the scrawniest one not two blocks distant, yellow street-lit,
yellow even without the snowcapped streetlight, for all
I know yellow on a moonless, starless midnight.
In which there is an infinite number of streets to choose.
But this chronically deformed hanger-on leaf with its shoulders scrunched
isn't looking special, winter is heavy-early,
a din all crow and over the top, and the leaf curls
beginning at the tips until it is crouched
deep into itself and feels your pain, readers, you bookish birdbrains,
all you crows have its face, every one of you early this year.
It's usually late February when you royal pains-in-the-back,
you critics of carrion, settle as crows on the oaks.
I never see you first I always hear you first,
mistaking you for some mechanical noise,
like something man made up—Yeats said that man created
death and that was an unforgivable moment, even for Yeats.
Whereas you crows know both how to kill and how to die
but mostly just wing around and get nowhere new.
An hour later and into twilight what can there possibly
be to cry about so far and away outside
my body, out there where you know other tricks than I do.
You know how to open the trash bin, and only for a while
do the owl decoys work before you smarten up,
or dogs stalk you before you alight, pause, and sweep down.
I've waited too long to compare my spindly self to this leaf.

It is a senior without a walker or a hospice
I tore from the tree without the slightest sense of transgression
to be a bookmarker in a dictionary of affliction.
So many definitions of hyperaffect, so many crutches,
meds, zero gravity chairs, MRIs with their open
mouths and the blindfolds for terror and the long night
when you are not evil and you are not purposely
trying to torment me. There is a point
of reference here. Which is? My pain? It is not mine.
Oh sacrum and iliac, two wings keening out every step.
Whose bone on bone is there to hear in your screeches,
internalities clash with internalities in your scuffles up there,
I have the X-rays to show you, my heart looks like fog,
I can see the streetlights in that fog, the houses are those
I recognize, I live behind one of the warmer windows.
Anything I could have against you is not even mine
to offer but a leaf can truly be a heralded object,
it is not bronze decor but blinding as a tinfoil palace.
But I remember tin scares you as I open my arms to you
like a loving scarecrow on fire, please warm to my fire.
But I cannot make a home only an object for you,
the palace can have wings if I choose it to, or it can fold
to a tinfoil boat to sail to Charon and Dis and beyond,
where the fathers get you all to eat out of their hands.
I do not have any offering, only this leaf—
when all you want is peanuts, like the mountain jays.
You are all opera stars but you just want peanuts, a watermelon rind,
a fry, half a hot dog bun and for all I know
you are tired of mimicking our human voices.
You only begrudgingly make pets and only okay pets.
You alight as the black angel on my father's shoulders.
He put a peanut there and he now lives behind a gate.
Where there should be rifle towers but there is only a
a lazy guard watching TV and his panel of red buttons.
Whereas you live outside and not in carrels or attics like readers.

And not in the worldwide net or in the cloud.
And sometimes you warn one another of me.
And me and my likes, we hurry toward everything.
What else descended from the crown to the roots?
The trees, their buried grasp, their darkening of the heavens.
I just want to hear out some rustle of my own litter
from the pig-out of affliction, and stay minor and livable
and shun the epochal and the heroic or citizenly.
In fact, my affliction doesn't write poetry at all,
I cheat you each and every one by putting you down,
sleep doesn't do so well by me, I can't always sleep to wake.
Pain is a pebble one of you crows drops into
the pitcher, another, another, soon the water
reaches the level of your beak and you drink.
Aesop caws a fable. The moral is the usefulness of pain . . .
All well enough but twilight's strife is amoral.
Your midair jousting is what twilight brings,
knives you cut for yourselves from stiff stalks of grass,
nuts you drop onto black asphalt till one of our cars
crushes them open for you, fifty miles each day
you spending your time mostly alone flying solo for food before
your funnels and gathering uproars twilight brings,
and I must accept that you don't cry like black angels
or like a leather coat on fire, or a leper hit by a hearse.
Shiny as you are, as familiar as we hear the sight of you
you are not even shoes, you are not even bastards
though you can be bastards to one another,
the oddly acting one among you often attacked
by all you others because the murder matters
more than the weak, and the injured attract predators.
A little white on the wing is okay. Ten thousand
of you crows of the tree of heaven winter has stripped
just so each of you can be an abundant leaf.
Just who I am to offer you this spindly bookmarker
while you are cold, goddamn miserable, some of you

are starving, others of you pointlessly infirm,
you outcasts you easy targets that draw hawks.
Yes too many white markings and you can forget it.
God knows how many of you are virtually
out of your minds from another harsh season.
Not even God can know what pointless cruelties,
what abject distances devoid of possibilities,
what carcasses fallen from heaven without a proper burial,
what hunters in the snow what hoarders what
desperate abominations what avaricious sinkholes
what coal clinkers, devious sheens, what miscreants.
You, you, you, I stutter, I can't help you, or myself.
Take this leaf, my favorite, and tear it to less than a shred.
You and your ingratiating pecking orders, loathsome
self-loathers, there is blood on your ingrate minds
running from your mouths and flooding the valleys,
resentment in tongues that sometimes I understand.
Today is clearing I do not know whose throat.
That this object, this objective, this offering . . . is.
I'm trying to think of all the right words at once,
scrunching up my face, my best hope in action.
Isn't such pain a redoubtable language of blank
that "cannot recollect," as Dickinson said,
a language discrediting the usual pieties—hey,
you others—pain of you others even my loved ones
I so readily turn away from, reeling, so I can feel
my pain from a distance while the trees you land in
some are birch and look arthritic but most
are oaks and flex their branches and mesomorphic trunks.
Roots and rhizomes downward deeper than the taproot.
The pain, as Paul Monette wrote of a time "before AIDS,"
is chronic, not a flower or seeds or this leaf, but a root.
Pain "to school an Intelligence and make it a soul" (Keats).
"A Place where the heart must feel and suffer in a thousand
diverse ways" (Keats again). Bitch-goddess Lamia's
"murmuring of love, and pale with pain" (yet again, Keats).

Pain of Saint Sebastian put to death because he chose
to bear it, arrows fashioned of tree shot through flesh.
Whereas you are arrows of blackness all day and all night,
you are your own afflictions, without which,
as Plato said, we would not consent to live,
you children of (Cioran) "the terror of being born,"
pain (Scarry) entailing your feelings of being acted upon,
pain that is not mine nor yours nor anyone's,
pain (Sharon Cameron) inevitable as suffering
is not nor ever will be if the work is beautiful.
In the neighborhood of snow you crows, you
crowing like a graveyard for the carved, once intimate names,
another dawn innocent of pain will be breaking out,
the light rising sooner than ever, all over again
a day without snow may never arrive, the path
up the hill with the snow-scabbed trees is an upwards sentence,
a sentence not mine any more than affliction is,
having left me to this separateness—"It feels like
an impaled pickax" and my wife—"I understand it."
You black-robed judges, I'm singing to the choir,
I must have a word to say to you and have it out
here in the open with you, take this leaf, and streetlights,
stay on, you're needed, if only for the night.
If I am out of words it's because the language
is an incalculable debt that is mounting like poverty.
Someone, burn all the leaves, but this one leaf.
I'm praying for it, too. It smarts, and has your smarts.
Crows, you should be praying for me, but I'm okay.
I'm praying pain forgives itself, as I just cannot,
I'm praying, not for the favor of some upscale Other.
For me, you, and the others, I'm praying for the words
that constitute all prayers, except the wordless prayer
after the one in words, the prayer that looks out
on silence in wonder once the crows have settled
down for another night to a less addressable realm
without a cry or whimper, or even a whisper.

Leafdom

These leaves are neither poems nor Whitman's hair.
Scuttling across sidewalk openly, whatever they mean.

No scented handkerchief, no hair of young men.
Nor of women, daughters or sons. Nothing ours.

The world below is where these leaves return.
They've fallen, and the ground is their heaven.

I have been there and you have and that's where
our fathers and mothers came from, and their ancestors.

From earth the stars rise, and quiet human gaze.
The stars come up like trees. They quiet words.

The leaves are not blood let of innocent childhood:
I can get over these leaves. Their deepening mess.

I can read practically anything into these leaves
but the isolate beauty of doing so can feel awful.

They have nothing to do with books or book burning
or Kindle or freedom fetishized by technology.

They don't know the summers are getting longer.
They have no idea. They can't even imagine us.

I could blame myself, but I'm not sure, that sounds
beneath human decency and beside the point.

I could fault the passage of time, but I'm not sure
I could find a God to believe me. And I could

go on taking these walks until these walks stop.
Life is unfair. That life is unfair is unacceptable—

that's the dumbfounded prayer behind poetry.

III

Marram Grass

Marram, from *Ammophila*. From the ancient Greek. Which is dead. Meaning no one lives anymore who knows how it sounds. But a dead language goes on like wind because it is still pushy and fundamental and yet invisible. Maybe the wind came first. Wherever the word came from, marram travels by benefit of wind over the lake, upon the lake the fright wigs of the rhizomes—shoots of roots taken up in ghostly matted clumps like a fine surprisingly gentle steel wool—bobbing in the light of cloud and lake all day and night until they meet an earthly night or an earthly day of sand and glacial silt John Muir called glacial flower. Wherever he now is, you can see this wind-woven grass of the ancients sunlit by day and moonlit by night. But the source of it here came in across the lake by virtue of wind. Of exile. As breath is exiled and exhaled into words. So marram is from the drift of root and the wind of all and any dead languages in this language of updraft and downdraft—the wind carries the sand, the water the roots. So out of water the roots beach to bind the sand and build the parabolic dunes because first things first including the truly beautiful.

Its fate is always to look like the first thing you've ever seen in your life. But it arrived before first. Before birth certificates. Before origin myths. Before "to be." In the beginning was the world. And then down under the sand that marram held and where it rooted, this grass casts a string net of fibers slender enough to confound a tweezers. These fibers hold the saltated fine sand in place below ground while above ground, where we walk and stroll or plow, wind blows the surface-creep of coarse sand. Bare hands cannot clutch a blade of it, bare eyes just go off walking water towards some lumbering barge with zebra mussels in its bilge. And then fog. And the first thing you see appear in the fog and windblown sand and then the windblown light of day is this grass that parted wind and condensed the fog into sequins of droplets and insinuated a way into the sand like the rain does—without eyes or hands.

This green woods is its living ghost. The living shade of the woods it makes possible kills it. The face of the deep and the darkness upon the duff floor. But a trail comes out to marram grass. It's in love with the sand, if not its own limits. It stabilizes the sand and its work is in the woods that follow and choke off its sunlight. And it is as the wind when it is windy. It is with the clouds. And it understands stars. And it is as a roar in the treetops. And if it looks tough, blades in plain sight, it is even stronger in its unseen, subterranean motile distillations in deed and fact, for which the way down is the way up because for marram grass there is no burial and no resurrection and no need for a Department of Resources or Father or Mother or Spirit on the Water or exceptionalist nations or global sing-alongs, its roots are tougher and far more diverse down here, below measure, thinner than hair where lively is deepest and finest.

It holds and is battered by each grain here on earth, which is the subconscious of our subconscious, only roots go down there (not even James Cameron goes down there), and though the deeper sand is fine, this surface sand is coarse and imperfect. Pocked like the moon and otherworldly if you put it under a microscope. I know this because my friend discovered my interest in sand and dune grass, my friend who blows in by e-mail now and then. She shot me a gallery of photos of grains all pitted all alarmingly asymmetrical and oblong and as scored and scarred as the surface of the moon up there tonight and forever and a day till hell and heaven and earth and all the dead and living languages pass.

That was the first time I saw a grain of sand up close and it looked like a bombarded planet that had lost the will to revolve and spin and suspend and that had been taken up with the windblown multitudes.

What beached first, grass or the beach? Which, grass or sand, was the first is like asking how we got here into our bodies. We blew in cell by cell. We got here from a long way, from under our feet and over our heads. To some inside we first appeared. Once out, all we made of ourselves in our own image ran amok. Marram infiltrated the sand without a backhoe. It held the sand first, the sand held it first. Such love is inhuman. And marram is of no value. Now the sand it held to is trucked away for foundry casting molds, road construction, winter road treatment, construction fill—the mining sites turned focal points for golf courses, condos, pods of starter mansions—Muskegon Sand Manufacturing. The grains, once windrowed, are now fired and melted and shaped into windows and windshields and test tubes and lenses and hand mirrors and closet mirrors and rearview mirrors and concave mirrors for observations in observatories that scour the sky in observance of the stars. But sand was the first—and the gray silt called glacial flower. And well before sand or marram or lake or even glaciers, wings crossed the blue sky that the lake bears up. And stars crossed the same at night. And the stars preceded night, for night is still young. What came first, day or night?

It was the first pilgrim, before peach pea blossom, sea rocket, cottonwood, jack pine, bluff face, perched dune, parabolic dunes blowout, tiger beetle, sanderling, sandpipers, sandhill crane, Marquette, Joliet, Joseph Strange (titular aptism) and his Mormon Stepford Wives on Beaver Island, Henry Ford, Cornish, Czechs, Germans, Norwegians, second generation locals—they used to bowl bowling balls down Empire's Front Street on New Year's Day—tourists (cone-lickers, fudgies, lakies), forklift, foglift. Before paragliders, props, medical heli's, 747s, 757s, F-16s. Before preservation clapboard farms on Point Oneida. Before lightning rods, new tin roofs, newly hewn barn planks. Before desuetude. Before restoration. Before nostalgia. Oneida Point: this is how America used to look—Natural Farmland, it's an outdoor museum. As far as the road can see are poles without fence. And a little white schoolhouse without its children, safe, vacant, nature as preservation, memory as preserve.

On dry days marram descends deeper. In driest weather it curls to a tube. The underside of the blade then forms the outer surface. Underside goes inside out and outer and the waxy coating reduces water loss, long roots to locate the water dissipated in sand. In the beginning was as if now. As if now drew the rain to the sand and the sand to our feet.

Wherefore the marram finally settled the land there also sprang the children who are as the sand in the sea, and houses on stilts as good as gone. Yet here to this day wash in all the revelations of all the nations which are from the corners of the earth and the number of which is as the sand of the sea and as many as the stars in heaven. Multitudes. And the sand, which is by inland glacier, and the shores, innumerable, endangered, and taken away by scenic road and path, and whatever remnant shall be saved is caught in the web and warp and weave of balding stretches of marram where the heron hides at twilight that sprang from the seed head. Which is open. Which has no skull. Which has no remembered present. Memory as in flesh, then, precoded and categorized memory the chaff of which is functional as and the rest of which is multifarious and continuous and revised and revisited as rain is revised by sand and sand is revisited by rain. Which arrives from clouds glaciers could have been. The foredune is eaten to an open shelf exposing marram root. Largely rhizome itself, fiber more than anything else, a cousin to wool, you can pull it out but it's hard to do that to it, it is so inextricable. And why would you wish to anyway? And at that the look goes up above the sand shelf. Not so much a path as a brook of sand that is beach spill from legions of feet leads up and back into the canopy, where our observations can again live the good life of myriad endless moods. Of the very first serenity. The very first author. Moods which critique and savage one another into a sense of territory precisely the way observant chickadees bicker in one place in the choked undergrowth. These observant chickadees are also forms water assumed. Water, fine and sensitive element, widespread element.

Thoreau said it that way. He died not long after he passed by here on his way back from Minnesota, where of all places in this nation of nations his lungs were to heal. He was also a form water assumed. Every successive liveliness gets taller towards light. All day on the beach are people at a distance, the words of whom cannot be made out. But the trees behind them and you watching as always the lake can be heard. You don't even have to turn around. The body understands these old green voices. The rustle can sound like the lake itself. It can rattle like the ghost of a whale. Up in the leaves without words wind is the throat that swallows us all.

Then the foredunes and then the troughs and the meadows and then the towering dunes and the walkways and the observation decks and the paraglider I saw above Sleeping Bear calling down to answer the ridiculous question how is it up there by saying heaven it is heaven up here while he blew around like a pilgrim without a country or a flagship or a home to call lost.

IV

A Natural History of Silence

Out of silence, out of fullness, out of a wave
that flatlines,
    there, a wing, breaking. Then other wings.
    Silence pools with its larvae in every word.
    The gnats climb out of silence.
    There are pools of water off to each side of the pencil-
yellow dirt road, the entire forest best underwater, so if
you look down,
    you see sky if the no-see-ums let you.

                          *

Silence came from earth like the trees you still climb
    with your childhood eyes that also crawl
    across the sky the earth thinks up
but is silence really where you want yourself?
    The silence of that . . . that childhood—
    knowledge of punishment, then shameless disbelief—
    and every day after the sky beginning to become
the creation again.
    In the original.
    There is no original.

                          *

The ancient Greeks thought "silence hides in the ground."
    It must be frightened, because it knows the moment it makes
itself heard it no longer exists.
    It is the ultimate gift, free of danger.
    Unlike the lyric poem, unlike Sappho's "broken tongue."

Birdsong that exists in the throat of its own extinction,
such is silence, a privilege only the rich can now afford.

*

You see birch trunks, slender spokes, unnegotiable.
They slim the light back into earth from which light
rose, like smoke, amazed.
Past the birch are the ghost orchard's outstretched
arthritic hands that clutch the fog that rose from coves.
The brook babbles like a baby on the verge of a first
word.
Words see up from mud the bursting trillium's
tricorn trumpet.
In every silence there is something of the spoken.

*

By 1866 theories of the origin of language were so numerous
that the Société de Linguistique de Paris refused to accept any
additional paper dealing with the topic.
By the even more annotated twenty-first century
you could stack the books on silence
all the way to the incognito moon's polycratered pall.

*

Subsequent theories of silence demolished their precedents,
which
withered like daffodils after an early frost,
for what mattered defied prior knowledge,
was the disappearance of the inarticulate . . .

*

Language rose out of drool, not silence. Before we spoke
a word
     we already knew how to hunt without a sound.
     In the human face was always something sad—
     the knowledge of the kill in advance of song.

                              *

Ominous silences often break out into cries the same
silences amplify,
     what the silence amplifies is crying from silence,
     and the silence of these silenced lives is crying
     of such poor streets, what a poor species with all
its houseless
     and that uproar of pandemonium in silent ears.

                              *

The void we think we grasp at, the old Beyond Words
lets go.
     The trees suspire, branches heave, the limbs rattling.
     Quiet again then rattle, wind which in itself is mute
     so far inside itself
     seems as nothing,
     just as anyone who in the Name of Silence called silence
an auditory delusion
     seems as nothing.
     All the greenest thoughts annihilate themselves.

                              *

The child imitates the mother imitating the child's
babble
     and the first language is born.
     The mother stops imitating the child and the child
starts imitating the mother

and the second language is born.
Steam glyphs rising from coves, sequined thorns and spiderwebs
gone diamond on themselves,
    figure becomes a found-and-found and the third and
    last and the second and the first language is silence.

*

To the extent that nobody is as calm,
    collected, deliberate, or composed as even the most agitated
sentence is,
    every speech act implicates a vehemence.
    These birch trunks are for a fly-by-night moonlight,
the homeless shadows, and vagrant wrens.
    Yet a word has its roots to clutch with,
    every description is a declarative act and every declarative
act
    is a vehemence.

*

If a tree in the forest should happen not to fall and no one
was there not to hear it not make a sound,
    did that tree make a silence? None you can hear.
Eyes among eyes we looked out from, one another's—
    you can't hear silence, you can only see it—
    in crocuses—pilot lights at our mute feet—
    as the light of day will have its live answer.

*

If you don't think much of small talk, try living without it
awhile.
    Then open a sentence that wishes to be spoken
    as friends, loves, family members, strangers do.

Stopping dead middle of a sentence is a tactic.

On a given day you may have been unaware you were feeling
like that
until you open your mouth for the first time all day,
trying to strike the others as you appear to yourself.

Unto

Far deep into early morning I actually start hearing the things
I hear,
    pen to ruled paper screeching faintly across that paper,
    the notebook itself squeaking, the ears always about to
open,
    soprano vireos, cardinals zring-zringing like anonymous voices
    sometimes did through slouching phone wires
    in the little of childhood not yet disconnected,
    it's the notebook talking—it's the notebook talking again—I'm not
going to say another word, I promise, quiet,
    I'm writing here, I can't speak to you, you're someone else,
    as these hands turning the pages in wild daylight are always
someone else's,
    someone who has never written a sentence in his life.

Seasons of the Day

About ourselves we know too much,
and we have talked creation half to death,
but I cherish going on in words.

A green leaf contained a gold leaf.
This is the one and only season of
this one and only waking hour and even when I listen,

even when I shut up I'm still shrill.
Dawn almost ceases to live and begins to be
the smallest of birds.

What season shall we name this distant waking hour?
What would be called spring when it's October all day,
and November would do us in?

A few hours into the done-and-gone a low-down
disgusted wind that doesn't know why it's windy
dies to an awareness of awareness.

Creepy. And the lake has nothing to say.
This season of cynical cresting smiles.
Another hour, another, ending in reflection if I'm standing

high enough on a bluff and above it all
taking in the panoramic dead-reckoned
desolate waves that are always in season.

What season of the day did I feel no self-pity,
never begrudged friends their loveliness,
never slandered a single person

out loud or in my angelic heart,
and never despised my beloved
for being gentler than I will be.

It is not my weakness before others I despise,
not hatred that hangs me out to dry.
Quiet village avenues, I listen in, too.

I can almost hear the light fall asleep.
Tree shade shallows to twilight
and a deer not fawn but not yet a yearling looks up,

the look of this deer says with perfect mercy
get your own twilight and invisibility,
be busy right now with your own story.

I'm sitting in a booth of a place called Friendlys.
Old friend I haven't seen in decades.
We have seen our own way to seating ourselves.

I find myself in the company of words.
My friend ending an astonishing story
is suddenly stricken, ashamed by his own enthusiasm.

In the last season of the day he finishes the story, it's real.
A guy in a lifeboat catches a seagull that lands on his head
after an eternity lost in the Pacific.

I'm eating my literal fries.
I have no idea who this person really is anymore.
This is the season of memory and leave-taking and

he looks old when his voice says old and old says
It'd be a wonder if I made it to 85.
Yeah and then you look around and really wonder.

130 seconds or 130 years of consciousness—
it's a miracle that we are even talking.
One day we won't know which of us said what.

Now one of us is going on about some new theory
about the universe being finite
because infinity, a limited concept,

is only human.

Leafdom

Yellow across rat-gray asphalt—blue sky up there—patches—
no—not patches—openings—amorphous—tatters—
as blasted and frantic as clouds—as shaken trees—as me—
like as not of no use whatsoever—
like as not to lead to false conclusions—
what apprehensions—what distractions—the rest of life and death this one leaf—
this day—never—not yet . . .—finished,
this sentence—far from complete—far from it—
one leaf blown across road—
no longer shaking up there—
far from it—

Ceasing Never

To chronic pain

The cricket is the only eco-poet. Thoreau knew it. And Keats. James Wright, his bones emerald with envy. And how. It posits a creak here and there, even by day, come fall, which is as a long twilit summer. It is compact enough to be honest. It is unaware of the water skimmers and their little watery flying trapeze wire caliper traces on which they seem to hang for life. It cheeps. Without it the very universe above would be as quiet and pious as a Sunday morning, as hushed as the creek bed with pebbles wide as faceless mouths and ventrifacts from lag zone's friable cobble of pebble and ultrafine sands which saltate—quartz, feldspars, calcite, garnet, hornblende—but a cricket is no linguistic miner, it is the wood's town crier.

I diagram in observance to you these diminutions these particulates these finest magnetites all treasure trove, though silt tracks like oil spill. I diagram for you the freshet Otter Creek, a compound sentence artery'd and papillary'd by dependent runlets, all of them corpuscle'd by minnows. But does the diagram drop to its knees when I cry out loud from you, chronic Pain—do I cry or do I sing of a day as long as a great lake is wide—should I—and why ask you? Is this what you keep saying, why ask?—what kind of question is this?—Here, I'm talking Here—Pain, Big Shot Pain, intimate you, Pain, anonymous you, dunderheaded you, well-intentioned but overreaching messenger, I conflate you with a cricket creaking like an open door. Why would you want to listen? Why would I wish to kill you both?

I had been adulating the cricket but does the cricket have any idea where the other shore is, let alone this one? Clouds slide right off its chart. The sky is beyond scope or coping with. Pain, I give you a little more thought than I ought for anyone's sake, I give you the creeps, I give you laryngitis, and then I just look dumbly and say here, there, there, calm down. Thoughts, you can shallow even if—to—sedge—deep enough—great lake carrying heaven on its back as if heaven were a light burden all the while this cricket alongside a crooked creek is winding down. It is exactly this easy to die.

Green Flash

As the sun sets it dims to a stage-light brightness you can gawk at, but the crinkled light on crinkled lake is the greater miracle. With such slick watercolor you actually feel kinship. The orange of sunset on water is a deluge of fire. The sun could be a sphere of flesh. Then the glimpse I'd waited many dusks out for. Contingencies: clean air, mirage, refraction. Just so. Reaching the observer without being shredded or scattered. It isn't much more than the afterimage would be if the gaze at a green flame were suddenly to turn to a white wall, or if we simply closed our eyes. Which is to say this green flash isn't how dusk works at all. Dusk dilates the most open eyes. What this one instant of a day hospitable to memory amounts to is a minuscule crescent on a pinhead. You don't have to strain to see it, but it isn't going to lead to an expansive consciousness. The sun sets first, then its jeweled special effect is something you know you are seeing for the first time and the last time. As a surprise. As a good-bye. And such a precious good-bye has to happen within the instant before the disappearance that sponsors the good-bye. That's it. The sun having set, every stone sets, every pebble, the narrow beach, verge milkweed, west-facing house sides, straggler skateboard kids high-fiving and reaching above their heads to heaven to do so, a tortoise ride on springs, the rusting space rocket with the rusting spiral staircase, the parking spaces where cars were, empty green benches, any memory of who was sitting on them, even the absences that have been invented out of some desire that life be otherwise.

Coyote after Field Fire

Of all the urban myths that feed on weakness,
the coyote has some meat to it, it bears itself, it takes it slow,
it takes it down whatever it is,
  it is the gift
  that jugulates the giver in its tracks
  and eats until the myth is anorexic.

———————

Messed-over animal is what it is.
It chews and swallows until its very thoughts are wholly
digested,
  it walks forth on blackened feet, then crumples to controlled burn
with not even grasshoppers grazing,
  it looks as lost as glut,
  it lifts its head up to being looked at.

———————

Only after it begins to die—
who needs a myth for this—
does it lower its inarticulated, delectable eyes
and bare its teeth at earth.

———————

It is said to howl but it doesn't even sob,
not even after it throws off
flesh and bones does it sob,
  not even after it is taken back by earth to a place of
further-than-ever
  and its ribcage cradles the sooth and the pitiful poison
of a wasp,
  which lights on it, and pauses eternally . . .

Up There

Gulls, you may see all we do, but I live under the clouds in my writing, too, I live in a fishbowl down below you, here with the lowly leaves. I am as private as an animal. And that I am leads out to the walk across the wooden bridge with the warped new planks and the tree shade that was like breath from the ground that had soaked up the rain after a drought and the breath was a half-life and cool on a hot night and a gladdening to cherish. What do you know of where we live down here with the shadows? How would you have us console ourselves? What does it mean not to have to survive the consciousness that the world may end? Not to miss a beat or a french fry? To cry like babies and tear the sky to rags? I wish I knew your mothers and your fathers before you. I wish I could fly like that. Just float around like purpose was a million lives away. But I know it isn't like that. I allow that brutality is the language of your ancestors. I defer to your precise savagery, and though people call you trash birds what do they know of nature except that they like it sanitary and time and place and mortality cleared like litter off the scenic path. Then you glide over a rickety bridge someone repaired on the cheap I only cross and it's not a river but traffic down there. And if there is weather to it, it doesn't knock us about. Who knows where you take shelter. It isn't heaven.

Frost at Dawn

Far down below black, lowest regret,
deeper than death, and deeper yet,
down where my mother weeps to me
to leave tomorrow's sorrows be,

far below sadness and tenderness,
where more is less and less is less,
below the sky or the sky-blue lake
brimming over like the hull of a shipwreck,

below where the crows crow and the cows sleep,
below the bluestem and the apples the cows crap,
below the prettiest sunset,
below even the bluest white-

bright-last-sunlight upon even bluer waves
gleaming their overly precious granite graves,
below funereal vacuities,
extravagant superfluities,

far below the lovers' quarrels,
or their story's broody morals,
in its own good time, time has gone back home.
Time and again, homeless time—

all the time in the world to be homeless
in the homeless space of universe,
all the time that time might pass
inside a shiny timeless hearse—

far down below idling hopes,
below the learned astronomer's telescopes,
wherever it is leaves must fall
is neither my life nor my choice to call.

———————

Upon a few gnarled stunted vines
fall's first frost fairly shines,
mist rising up from fields while new minted frost
mummifies a shingle-sided house.

Here is a glittery homelessness
better acquainted with earth than with us.
All we are is less substantial,
all our fears, less substantial.

Dawn is ready and the heart is able.
Fear could not be less substantial.
I've had it with odes to dejection,
which is never more than the fear of rejection.

———————

So here's what frost isn't—insubstantial,
querulous, of itself too full,
a mood of ferried buried
waves and the threadbare eroded

dunes we sightseers climb up and down to ruin.
Torment never spread itself this thin.
Incandescent, heartless, so like tin—
gull-gray gulls shriek atonal tunes.

The light of frost is the understudy of day,
this lake, once, as hard as rock:
icebergs—like ships, they broke
to floes that down on their luck

drowned, to nothing—invisibly.
This frost is anything but free.
It looks like the moonlight got good and lost.
It got busted, sprung, and lost.

Frost has a cryological conscience:
the afterworld is cold chance.
Lunatical . . . white as a grin.
It shines unapproachably, like sunlight shines on tin,

whitening fields between cars and houses.
Plow-slashed furrows freeze
over smooth to its silver sky.
Forgive this intricate analysis

but it looks so stunned and incredulous.
It is spotty, like a roof of a vacant crystal palace.
Instantaneously tenuous,
it scribes the window glass.

———————

It is so distinct from rain.
It shuns asphalt as too human.
The lustrous is
incipient in us.

Its deposition of glory
is inexplicably ordinary.
What a tenacious
underside of heaven it is—

it won't be pushed around or salted or plowed like snow.
It won't be tracked on and no weatherman will see it lift.
It is profligate thrift.
Its past is vaporous.

Beauty never spread itself so thin—
incandescent, the heartless night
turned inside out—
pasture field light.

———————

The great lovers once frantic to touch
in darkness no dawn or frost can reach—
my mother gone in the blink of an eye,
my father going by and by,

all mothers, all sisters, all fathers, all sons,
all brothers and keepers, everyone's
truest, best, lost influences,
nameless lovingkindnesses . . .

it is all and none of this.

———————

It seems irretrievably early.
Time is awake, only barely,
infinitesimal hates,
infinitesimal fights.

Tight, fibrous, and delicate,
around the fine white plow-bared roots,
its extremely minute white
threads appeared overnight.

It prompts us and then reproves us.
Its intricate paralysis
crystallizes . . . miraculous.
Preposterous. Analogous.

———————

The leaf falls to earth and keeps
falling and cups the frost,
then decomposes beyond the deeps,
to teach us how to be lost.

———————

So night may be said to be over,
over, and over at no real cost,
each dawn the stars take cover.
Stop fretting about the frost.

Frost clung to the shadow places
and as always already was there
before anyone could take a step.
In the sky, stars stayed on

while you were asleep.

———————

While you were asleep
everyone was asleep;
if we sleep, if we die,
stars hang in the sky.

Between our houses
is its heartlessness,
but whatever grass
is, the frost blesses

whoever sees this,
whoever would mean
that frost be seen
not heard in this:

now fields steam and
its steam mists to sky.
Under us is only sand
and who can say why,

or whose voice this is.

And the Creatures Lay Down

The woods running out of breath
were paradise, you and I
rocking in sex like kids on swings,
trying out open tunings
or whatever we wished that seemed pure
and apart from our parents
and all humankind, and now
the ice caps are on the verge
of a nervous breakdown,
it's time our generation said
good-bye. That bowling ball
in my hands was my head,
before even midnight died
there was lots of wind to listen lost to
but when it lightninged
one beautiful sight was you.

And the world was just like
a reality and mostly ours to
kite alongside our loved ones
hurled like birds by the wind
beak first into the mortuary.
We stopped crying at the sad parts
to cry at the joyous parts,
then turn to one another.

Saint Lucy's Night

That houselight, lowest star. The leaf blowers are quiet. The longest sentences have all abated. This one day ends at midnight, like all the rest. Ordinary nothing John Donne said. There are books all over the house, most closed, a few open. The mind is so small that the heart cannot pronounce it.

Notes

"Posthumous Cabin": "what God shat," an adaptation of "god-shit," a term translated from the Pussy Riot song "A Punk Prayer." Nadezhda Tolokonnikova, the nominal leader of the group, described "god-shit" as state-sanctioned religious fundamentalism that defiles any understanding of god.

"One Question for Ed": Edward Eimers, 1923–2009.

"Damnation": Francis Bacon's *Figure with Meat* hangs in the Art Institute of Chicago. The Joker of *Batman* (1989) was played by Jack Nicholson.

"The Afterlife of Deer" (p. 19–20): The Key deer is native only to the Florida Keys and is the smallest subspecies of deer.

"TechnoRage": This poem draws on diverse sources, especially *Against the Machine: The Hidden Luddite Tradition in Literature, Art, and Individual Lives*, by Nicols Fox. "Technorage" is said to describe decidedly human behavior: 80 percent of computer owners have at one time or another screamed obscenities at their computers; 50 percent of computer owners have inflicted damage to their computers. The definition of technorage can be reversed, under the assumption that any technology used for corporatizing or utopian ends rages against all forms in nature but the human form and, ultimately, against the human form as well.

"Under a Rainbow": The epigraph is from a song by Michael Burkard. I am indebted to two lines of Galway Kinnell's.

"Early Murder": Various readings on the subject of pain helped sponsor the poem, but the most crucial was from *The Culture of Pain* by David B. Morris: "We must begin to proliferate the meanings of pain in order that we do not reduce human suffering to the dimensions of a mere physical suffering . . . Indeed, the new thinking that lies ahead . . . when we learn what pain can teach us . . . may just lead to a future worth the pain it takes to create."

"Leafdom" (p. 52): The *Oxford English Dictionary* defines "leafdom" in the 1971 edition as "the realm of leaves" and in the most current edition as "foliage, especially when constituting a world of its own."

"Marram Grass": Sparse pockets of this North Atlantic grass can be found along the shores of the Great Lakes. *Ammophila*: from the Greek roots *ammos* and *philia*, "love of sand."

"A Natural History of Silence": This poem draws from, among other sources, *The World of Silence*, by Max Picard, the first full-length treatment on silence in English. "In every silence there is something of the spoken" is his sentence.

"Seasons of the Day": I have in mind Thoreau's phrase as it appears in *The Journal*: "What shall we name this season—this very late afternoon, or very early evening, this severe and placid season of the day?"

"Ceasing Never": A legal definition: chronic, permanent, perpetual. For a living definition, see Keats's "On the Grasshopper and Cricket."

"Green Flash": Also called "green ray," it is the rare optical phenomenon that occurs just after sunrise or just before sunset.

"Saint Lucy's Night": Saint Lucy is the saint of the blind: the day of the winter solstice, the least light-informed day of the year, is Saint Lucy's Day.